-Witchblade Takeru-
Story- Yasuko Kobayashi
Art - Kazasa Sumita
Original Comic by Top Cow Productions

TAKERU MANGA VOL. 2

Witchblade Created by Marc Silvestri, Brian Haberlin, David Wohol, and Michael Turner

Comic Artwork by Kazasa Sumita

Manga written by Kazasa Sumita

Script by Yasuko Kobayashi

Translation by Shoko Oono

English Script Adaptation by Brian Buccellato

Production by Team Pokopen

Edited by Robert Place Napton

Publisher Ken Iyadomi

Special Thanks Matt Hawkins

Originally Published by Akita Shoten

First Bandai Entertainment Inc version SEPTEMBER 2007
Printed in Canada

10 9 8 7 6 5 4 3 2 1

Chapter 6 Truth Revealed

THE PENTAGON
THE OPERATION IS BEGINNING TO BEAR FRUIT, RALEIGH.
I TOLD YOU THIS OLD PROJECT WASN'T A WASTE OF TIME.

CONGRATULATIONS, SIR.
NOT YET. NOT UNTIL I SEE IT FOR MYSELF.
カチャ clack
カチャ clack
カチャ clack
カチャ clack
IT'S CONNECTING.
GOOD...

HELLO... I'M SO HAPPY TO FINALLY MEET YOU!
SO, YOU'RE-
...THE WITCHBLADE BEARER.
AM I RIGHT?

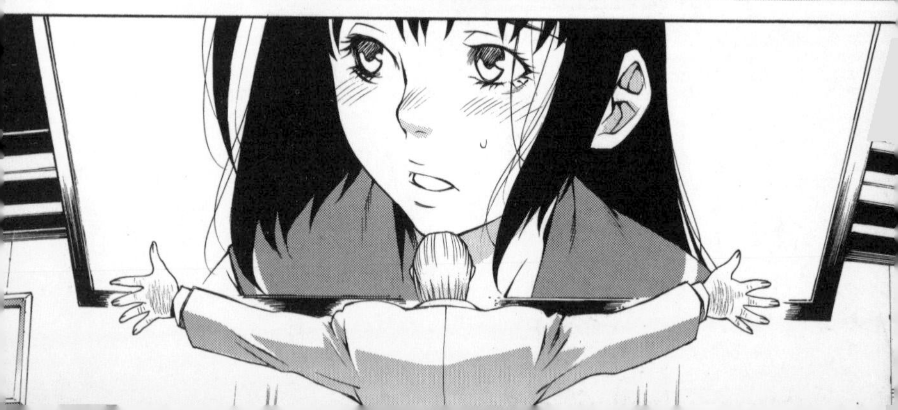

school the
ping the Secretary e
he guidance and forces
reign countries and our
naking serves as the pri
the President, the Sec
cial Security Offic
ject to law, power and
nsibilities include developin
wide financial policy, financia
gs and business modernizati
of the Joint Requireme
Chairman after
?
OH! RIGHT...
I FORGOT, SORRY.
HERE... FOR SIMULTANEOUS INTERPRETATION.
AHEM.

CAN YOU HEAR ME NOW?
I'M ERIC MASON, DEPUTY SECRETARY OF THE UNITED STATES DEPARTMENT OF DEFENSE.

DEFENSE?!
THAT... UHM... SOUNDS IMPORTANT.
OF COURSE IT IS!
HA, HA, HA, HA...
I ONLY RUN THE ARMY, NAVY, AIR FORCE, AND MARINES FOR THE GREATEST MILITARY FORCE ON THE PLANET.
WHILE I LOOK AT MEMOS FROM MOMMY, OF COURSE. HA, HA, HA, HA...
WHATEVER.

WE'VE BEEN SEARCHING FOR A LONG TIME.
FOR THE WITCHBLADE, OF COURSE.
AND THE HUMAN CAPABLE OF BEARING IT.
YOU ARE IN ELITE COMPANY, TAKERU.
RARIFIED AIR, INDEED. THERE ARE FEW WHO HAVE WHAT IT TAKES TO WIELD THE MIGHTY WITCHBLADE.

OVER THE YEARS WE GREW IMPATIENT, AND TRIED TO CREATE ONE OF OUR OWN.
BUT WHAT WE ENDED UP WITH...
WERE DEMONS.
?!
NO... POOR CHOICE OF WORDS.
IN TRUTH, WE ONLY "RESURRECTED" THEM.
WHATEVER MY CHOICE OF WORDS, THE RESULT IS THE SAME. DEMONS.

TAKERU IS WHERE?!
A CLASSMATE OF HERS TOLD ME THAT SHE WENT WITH KOU TO VISIT SISTER SEISHUU IN THE HOSPITAL.
BUT WHILE IN THE HOSPITAL, THE TWO OF THEM JUST UP AND DISAPPEARED.
THEY VANISHED OUT OF THIN AIR, DURING...
... SOME KIND OF "COMMOTION" AT THE HOSPITAL.

IT WAS DEMONS AGAIN!
THE DEMONS TOOK THEM!!!
WE DON'T KNOW ANYTHING YET...
DOCTOR...
DO YOU REMEMBER TWENTY YEARS AGO...
WHEN THE DEMON MOUND STONE WAS TOPPLED?
RIGHT... I REMEMBER LIKE IT WAS YESTERDAY.
WAIT! DO YOU THINK THAT WAS AN OMEN?
I DO.

SO YOU'RE SAYING YOU RESUR-RECTED...
DEMONS.
UNFORTUNATELY. YOU SEE, THERE IS A LEGEND...
...OF A DEMON'S HAND THAT EXISTED IN A CERTAIN MOUNTAIN VILLAGE IN JAPAN...
WHEN OUR RESEARCH DIVISION DISCOVERED THAT THE DEMONS DID IN FACT EXIST, WE PUT A COVERT TEAM TOGETHER...
AND WE SENT THEM TO INVESTIGATE.

AND...
THEY ENGAGED THE DEMONS AND EXTRACTED THEIR DNA.
AFTER MUCH TESTING AND RESEARCH...
OUR SCIENCE TEAM WAS ABLE TO RESURRECT THE EXTINCT DEMONS.
YET WE ALSO STUMBLED UPON SOMETHING OF PARAMOUNT IMPORTANCE.
THAT THERE WAS A WITCHBLADE BEARER AMONG THE DEMONS.
HOWEVER...

WE PAID THE PRICE FOR OUR RESEARCH. THE SHEER BRUTALITY OF THE DEMONS WAS BEYOND ANYTHING WE COULD HAVE IMAGINED.

IT'S ALL YOUR FAULT!
THERE WERE NO SURVIVING DEMONS!!!
WHY?!
WHAT WAS THE POINT ?!

S-SO, THOSE DEMONS TAKERU FOUGHT...
WERE YOU GUYS RESPON-SIBLE-
THEY WERE EITHER THE ONES THAT ESCAPED THE FACILITY... OR THEIR DEMON KIN.
WE DON'T KNOW HOW, BUT THEIR NUMBERS ARE GROWING.
HEY!

A GHASTLY TRAGEDY.
THERE WERE NO SURVIVORS.
SO WE SHELVED THE PROJECT, WITH NO INTENTION OF EVER REOPENING THAT PANDORA'S BOX.
I DOUBT EVEN THE JAPANESE GOVERNMENT KNOWS WHAT WE DID.
NATURALLY, WE CLASSIFIED EVERYTHING...
HIDING ALL EVIDENCE OF THE EXISTENCE OF DEMONS.

THEY DESTROYED OUR RESEARCH FACILITY, AND SAVAGELY KILLED MY MEN. AND WHEN THEIR BUTCHERY WAS FINISHED... THEY VANISHED.

WHY THE HELL DID YOU BRING BACK THE DEMONS?!
IF NOT FOR YOUR MEDDLING...
TAKERU WOULDN'T HAVE HAD TO BECOME A BLOOD-THIRSTY....
KOU...

YOU'RE KOU MINAMOTO, RIGHT?
THE ONE WITH THE SWORD THAT KILLS DEMONS...
I WOULD REALLY LIKE YOUR COOPERATION ALONG WITH TAKERU.
COOPER-ATION? ON WHAT?!
WHY DEMON HUNTING...
OF COURSE!

TAKERU...
YOU WILL DO IT, WON'T YOU? YOU HAVE TO.
DON'T YOU SEE...? THIS WILL BE REVENGE FOR YOU.
WHAT?!
YOUR FATHER WAS THE ONE SUPERVISING THE RESURRECTION OF THE DEMONS.
!!
YES, YOUR FATHER.
HE WAS MURDERED BY THE DEMONS.

MASTER HOUGAN...
CAN YOU HEAR ME? IT'S FUURA.

FORGIVE ME, BUT I COME BEARING BAD NEWS.
THE WITCHBLADE YOU DESIRE... HAS BEEN STOLEN AWAY.
UHNGG..
UGHHH...
MY THOUGHTS EXACTLY.
IT WAS THOSE AWFUL AMERICANS.

BUT DON'T WORRY YOUR PRETTY LITTLE HEAD ABOUT IT.
THANKS TO YOU, MASTER HOUGEN...
WE HAVE AN ARMY OF DEMONS.
STILL, THE OUTCOME IS NOT CERTAIN.
WE ARE AT A SLIGHT DISADVANTAGE DEFENSIVELY.

GAKURA.

WE MUST RELOCATE. YOU WILL TAKE CHARGE.
YES....
RELOCATE?! WHERE?
WELL...
I THINK OUR BIRTHPLACE WILL DO QUITE NICELY.

AS YOU WISH.
BUT BEFORE YOU UNDERTAKE THIS IMPORTANT TASK, TAKE SOME OF MASTER HOUGEN'S STRENGTH.
YES, LADY...
UGH... UNGG...
HE HE...
OH...
LUCKY YOU...
IT SEEMS YOU GET TO HAVE A WHOLE LEG!

COME NOW...
RECEIVE YOUR SHARE.
MY LADY, I AM...
MOST GRATEFUL.
GUH... GUH
GUH... UNGH....

WOOSH!

YOU CAN REST IN HERE...
THERE'S ANOTHER BED IN THE NEXT ROOM. WHY DON'T YOU GET SOME SLEEP BEFORE THE MILITARY ESCORT GETS HERE?

THE MILITARY ESCORT ?!
BUT WE'RE WITH THE MILITARY NOW, AREN'T WE?
THIS BUILDING BELONGS TO THE NSWF.
THE WHAT?
THE NSWF... IT'S A GLOBAL WELFARE ORGANIZATION.
YOU'VE SEEN THE COMMER-CIALS, HAVEN'T YOU?

THE NSWF SUPPORT "THE FUTURE OF--
--MAN-KIND"!

OH...

AND I AM THEIR CHIEF RESEARCHER.
IT WAS ALSO THE NSWF THAT ORIGINALLY POSSESSED THE WITCHBLADE,

WHAT ?!

IT WAS AN ESSENTIAL PIECE OF RESEARCH MATERIAL AS WE EXPLORED THE LATENT POTENTIAL IN PEOPLE.

OF COURSE, WE HAD NO ONE WHO COULD ACTUALLY BEAR IT.
YOU WERE CHOSEN BY THE WITCHBLADE.
THAT WAS WHEN WE DISCOVERED THE TALE ABOUT THE DEMONS. SO WE DECIDED TO WORK TOGETHER WITH THE MILITARY.
AND HONESTLY, I CAN'T WAIT TO SEE WHAT KIND OF ABILITIES YOU HAVE. I LOOK FORWARD TO WORKING WITH YOU!
WELL, YOU SHOULD GET SOME SLEEP.
UH...
UHM...
YES?

THIS...
CAN'T YOU GET IT OFF OF ME?
WHAT?!
I... I WANT TO GET THIS OFF...
I DON'T WANT TO BECOME A DEMON!!!
SIGH.

OH, PUH-LEASE! YOU WONT BECOME A DEMON.
SO A DEMON FROM A LOOOOOONG TIME AGO ONCE WIELDED IT...
THERE'S NO REAL CONNECTION BETWEEN THE WITCHBLADE AND DEMONS.
WHAT ?!
IT'S NOT CONNECTED TO THE DEMONS?!
CLICK!
HON-ESTLY...
I'VE NEVER HEARD OF ANY PAST BEARERS TURNING INTO DEMONS.
......
BUT... THAT WAS...
CHIEF SAKURAI.

WHAT IS IT? YOU LOCATED THEM IN KIKAKUSHI VILLAGE?!

HUH ?!

HMM...
ドン
BOOM
BOOM
ドン
TI-KA
ドック
BOOM
ドン
BOOM
ドック
BOO
ドン
BOOM
ドン
BOOM

BA-BOOM
BA-BOOM

TI-KA
TI-KA

THIS WILL BE YOUR FIRST TIME COMING INTO OUR HOME, WON'T IT MASTER HOUGEN?
UHNG ...
UGH...
GUH...
YES... THERE IS SO MUCH TO LOOK FORWARD TO.

UH... UGH...
AH... UNGH...
GUH...
NO, NO...
YOU MUST NOT DIE.
NOT YET, MASTER HOUGEN.

BOOM
HEY, WAIT!
HOLD ON A SECOND!
THEY'RE GOING AFTER GRANDMA! I'LL NEVER... NEVER LET THEM TOUCH HER!
I'LL PROTECT YOU, GRANDMA! I'LL KILL THEM ALL!!!

CHAPTER 7 DEMON BLOOD

BOOM
BOOM
TAP
BOOM
BOOM
SISTER SENSHUU-NI...
BOOM

THEY'RE COMING BACK!!!
THE DEMONS HAVE RETURNED !!!
BOOM
DAMN IT...
BOOM
WOOOOSH
I'M CALLING THE MAYOR-
CLICK

YOU ARE A DOCTOR, CORRECT?
GOOD. THERE IS SOMEONE I WOULD LIKE YOU TO EXAMINE.

BOOM
BOOM
BOOM
TAP
BOOM
BOOM
BOOM
AAAAAHGLGHK!!!

GLGGHHH...
CHOMP... CHOMP...
クチャクチャ

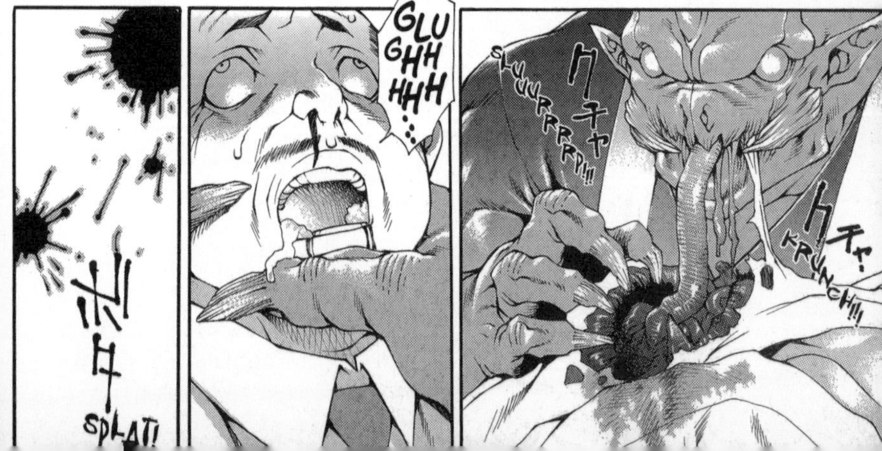

GLUGHHHHH...
クチャ
SLUUURRRRP!!!
クチャ
KRUNCH!!!
ボト
SPLAT!

TAP
BOOM
BOOM
BOOM
HUH?
AAAAAAAAAYYYYYYIIIIIIII!!!!
AAAAAAAAAHHHHHHHHH!!!!!

IT'S NO USE... THE PHONES ARE DOWN.
HUH?!
AAAAAAAAAAAHH!!!

PLEASE... TELL THEM TO FEED IN MODERATION.
AND COLLECT THE VILLAGERS IN ONE PLACE BEFORE THEY'RE ALL EATEN.
YES, SIR.
OH, AND MAKE SURE TO SEPARATE THE YOUNG WOMEN.
LADY FUURA WILL CERTAINLY ASK FOR THEM.
AS YOU WISH.
SHALL I HAVE SOME OF THEM PREPARED FOR YOU AS WELL, MASTER GAKURA?
NO NEED.
I'M A VEGETARIAN.

KRASH!!!
KRACK-AH
AAAAAAAAAAAAAAAAAAAH!

I'LL TAKE THIS ONE...
WAIT! WE SHARE... HALF AND HALF.
uh....
oh...
DRIP DRIP..

FINE...
BUT I GET TO SPLIT HER...

WITCH-BLADE!
HUH?!
BUT HOW... WHY IS SHE HERE?!

YOU... WERE TAKEN BY THE HUMAN MILITARY.
LEAVE MY VILLAGE...
NOW.
FOOL! THIS WAS OUR VILLAGE FIRST!

SLIKKKKT!

AAH...
OHHH...
SOB SOB
SNIFF... OH..
......

HMM... NO ONE'S ANSWERING.
HEY! PULL YOUR PANTIES UP!
I WONDER IF THEY FOUND TAKERU-CHAN AND KOU-KUN YET.
MAYBE I'LL STOP BY ON MY WAY HOME.

HONESTLY, I WOULD HAVE PREFERRED NOT TO FIGHT...
BUT SOME THINGS ARE UNAVOIDABLE.

STILL, I NEVER EXPECTED THE MILITARY TO ACTUALLY DISPATCH THE WITCHBLADE ONCE THEY FINALLY GOT THEIR GREEDY LITTLE HANDS ON YOU.
I SEE...
I CAME BECAUSE I WANTED TO. NO ONE DISPATCHES ME.
WELL, I WOULD APPRECIATE IT IF YOU WOULD NOT INTERFERE WITH MY BUSINESS.
INTERFERE ?!
I'M GOING TO KILL YOU.

I NEVER IMAGINED...
...THAT THE BEARER WOULD BE SO *BEAUTIFUL.*

OH MY...
DRIP DRIP...
YOU SEE, I NEED HIM ALIVE.
MASTER HOUGEN MUST NOURISH US WITH HIS FLESH AND BLOOD FOR A LONG TIME TO COME.

YOU'VE BEEN EATING HIM?!

TELL ME DOCTOR...
IS THERE ANY WAY YOU CAN REBUILD HIS ARMS AND LEGS?
UNGH...
NO! WHAT THE HELL ARE YOU, CRAZY?!
GASP!
UNBELI-EVABLE...
UNGH ...
WHAT IS IT THAT YOU WANT?!
WHY ON EARTH HAVE YOU DISTURBED OUR QUIET LITTLE VILLAGE.
UGH ...

THIS "QUIET LITTLE VILLAGE" IS SURROUNDED BY MOUNTAINS ON THREE SIDES, MAKING IT CONVENIENT TO DEFEND.
DAD?! GRANNY?!
BESIDES, THIS IS OUR HOME.
DAMN IT!
YOUR HOME?
THEN... YOU REALLY ARE THE DEMONS FROM THE LEGEND.

THAT'S RIGHT.
WE'VE BEEN RESUR-RECTED...
THANKS TO MASTER HOUGEN.
THAT MARK! OH MY, CAN IT BE?!
THAT THIS THING THEY CALL HOUGEN IS REALLY...

YES SIR, SHE LEFT OUR CUSTODY WHEN SHE HEARD HER VILLAGE WAS UNDER ATTACK.
AND I JUST RECEIVED AN UPDATE FROM OUR STAFF...
SHE IS CURRENTLY ENGAGED IN COMBAT WITH THE DEMONS.
THIS IS BAD, DEPUTY SECRETARY.
WE HAVE TO STOP HER, IMMEDIATELY.
WHY? SHE HAS THE WITCHBLADE.
OH, NO...
ALL OF THE DEMONS ARE CONVERGING ON THE VILLAGE!
EVEN THE WITCHBLADE COULDN'T POSSIBLY SURVIVE--

HA HA HA!
COME ON, NOW...
THE WITCHBLADE ISN'T SOME HAND PUPPET THAT MOMMY MADE.
SIR?
BESIDES, I SUSPECT THAT THE WITCHBLADE'S POWER HAS NOT COMPLETELY AWAKENED YET.
THIS MAY BE OUR ONLY CHANCE.
WE MAY FINALLY BE ABLE TO TAKE POSSESSION OF OUR TRUE OBJECTIVE.
THANK YOU FOR THE UPDATE. GOOD WORK.
GOODBYE, NOW.
ZZZZTTTT—
WHAT ?!
WAIT, DEPUTY SECRETARY!!!

OUR TRUE OBJECTIVE ?!
THINGS ARE GOING TO GET HECTIC, RALEIGH.
THAT MEANS IT'S NOT THE WITCHBLADE!
ISSUE AN EXECUTIVE ORDER TO YOKOSUKA BASE TO BE ON COVERT STANDBY AS A TRAINING EXERCISE.
FULL READINESS ALERT FOR THE NIMITZ...
THE ENTERPRISE...
...AND THE RONALD REAGAN, SHOULD BE ENOUGH.

LET'S GET THE OPERATION STARTED!

CHING
CLANG!
SZZZZZING!
OKAY THEN...

YOU'RE SKILLS ARE TRULY IMPRES-SIVE.
INSTEAD OF KILLING YOU AND TAKING THE WITCH-BLADE...
WE SHOULD HAVE ASKED YOU TO JOIN US.
DON'T WASTE YOUR BREATH. I'LL NEVER BECOME SOME DEMON!
PERHAPS NOT...
IT'S NOT POSSIBLE FOR YOU TO "BECOME" ONE...
BECAUSE, MY DEAR... YOU ARE ALREADY A DEMON!

"AND I'VE NEVER HEARD OF ANY PAST BEARER BECOMING A DEMON."
THAT IS HER...
TRUE NATURE...
LIAR!
...TRUE NATURE.

YOU'RE HALF RIGHT...
BUT DEEP DOWN YOU ALREADY KNOW THIS.
ADMIT IT. YOU FEEL THE THIRST... THE DESIRE TO FEED ON HUMANS.
NO!
YOUR BLADE IS USELESS AGAINST ME.
IT CAN'T INFLICT ANY DAMAGE AGAINST MY BODY.
SNATCH!
NOW DO YOU UNDER-STAND?

CHOMP!
AND EVEN THOUGH I'M A VEGETARIAN...
I REALLY WANT TO TASTE YOUR FLESH.
OH!
CHUCK!
KRASH!
CLINK!
YOU'RE RIGHT...
I HUNGER FOR HUMAN FLESH...
I THIRST FOR HUMAN BLOOD.
AND I CRAVE ONE OTHER THING. I ALSO...

... LOVE THE FEELING OF KILLING MY ENEMIES!
AND IF IT FEELS THIS GOOD, WHY STOP NOW?
YOU DON'T HAVE TO IF YOU JOIN US.
THE U.S. MILITARY WILL BE HERE ANY MINUTE NOW.
YOU CAN KILL UNTIL YOU HEART'S CONTENT...
AND FEED ON THEM.
YOU ARE TRULY A BEAUTY TO BEHOLD ...
...SECOND ONLY TO LADY FUURA.
PLEASE... JOIN US.
WHO CARES WHAT HAPPENS TO THIS WORTHLESS LITTLE VILLAGE?

!!!
HUH ?!
CRACK!
IT'S... IMPOSS-IBLE!
YOU ASK WHO CARES ?!
I DO. EVEN IF I WERE A LOWLY DEMON...
THIS VILLAGE IS MY HOME. MY FAMILY'S HOME... YOU DEMONS WERE STUPID ENOUGH TO LAY YOUR HANDS ON THEM.
AND FOR THAT...
I WILL NEVER FORGIVE YOU.

KRACK!!!
UNGH!!!!
AAAAAAAAHHHHHH!
THUK!

GASP... GASP...
HACK!!!
DOESN'T.... MATTER... WHAT YOU SAY...
...HACK!
YOU ARE ONE OF US.
HALF YOUR BLOOD... IS DEMON BLOOD...

IT'S IN YOUR VEINS...
IT IS WHAT DREW THE WITCHBLADE TO YOU...
IT CAN'T BE... THERE'S DEMON BLOOD... IN ME?!

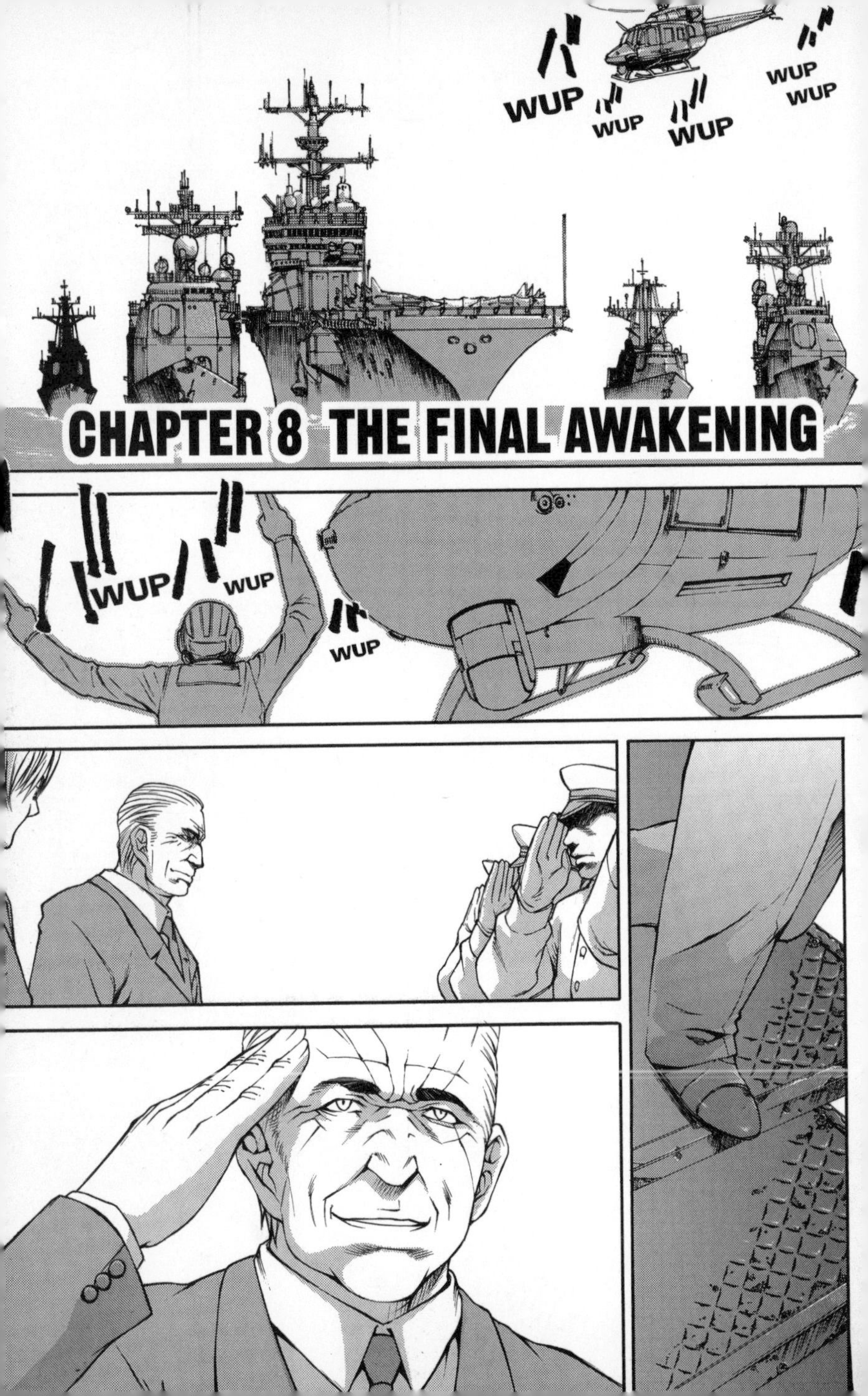
WUP
WUP
WUP
WUP
WUP
CHAPTER 8 THE FINAL AWAKENING
WUP
WUP
WUP

WE APPRECIATE YOU COMING ALL THE WAY OUT HERE TO INSPECT OUR TRAINING IN PERSON, DEPUTY SECRETARY, SIR.
I HOPE EVERYTHING IS UP TO SPEC. YOU WERE ASKED TO LOAD UP A GREAT DEAL OF FIREPOWER.
MOMMY'S GOING TO SCOLD YOU IF IT'S NOT UP TO SNUFF.
YES SIR!
IF THIS WERE A REAL WAR, WE COULD BLOW UP THE WORLD TWICE OVER.
VERY GOOD.
HOWEVER, LET ME CLEAR UP A MISCONCEPTION...
WHAT?
THE MISSION WE ARE ABOUT TO CONDUCT IS NOT A TRAINING EXERCISE.
IT IS A "REAL" WAR.

WHAT?!
SO THE UNITED STATES MILITARY IS GOING TO HUNT DEMONS?!
THAT'S UNHEARD OF, EVEN IN THE MOVIES!
THE U.S. NAVY IS MAKING A MOVE?!
MAYBE...
BUT IT'S A REALITY.
THIS IS GOING TO FAR...
IT'S BAD ENOUGH DEPUTY SECRETARY IS OBSESSED WITH HIS MOTHER, BUT THIS IS JUST INSANE.

AMERICAN FORCES ARE COMING?
YOU MEAN, **HERE**?!

WAR IS INEVITABLE.
SO WE WILL NEED TO RETAIN YOUR SERVICES FOR A LITTLE LONGER, DOCTOR.
IF THAT IS...
... THE MAN I THINK IT IS... THEN THIS IS TOO MUCH.
WHY WOULD THE AMERICANS...

SCRAPE ズル
ズル SCRAPE

TAKERU ?!
GAKURA !!!
LADY... FUURA...

TAK... TAKERU?
TAKERU-CHAN?!

TAKERU!
LET GRANDMA AND KOU'S FATHER GO... NOW.

YOU...
WOOSH!

THUD!
OH, GAKURA...
IT MUST HAVE BEEN... SO PAINFUL.
LADY FUURA...
I AM SO... SORRY...
TWITCH!
TAKERU...
WHY ARE YOU... LIKE THIS?

GRAND-
THUMP!
MA...
TAKERU!
GRANDMA...
I'M... A...
I'M HALF DEMON.
HE TOLD ME...
I HAVE DEMON BLOOD COURSING THROUGH MY VEINS.

NO.
WHAT?!
THERE IS NO WAY YOU ARE THE SAME AS US!!!
THE ONLY WAY YOU COULD DO SOMETHING SO BRUTAL...
...IS BECAUSE YOU ARE HUMAN!

WHO ARE YOU KIDDING?!
YOU DEMONS ARE THE ONES BRUTALLY FEEDING ON US!!!
HOW IS THAT DIFFERENT THAN WHAT YOU DO TO COWS AND CHICKENS?
EATING HUMANS IS NATURAL BEHAVIOR TO US.
SO YOU SEE...
WE ARE SUPERIOR TO YOU HUMANS, AFTER ALL.
WHAT?!
THAT'S RIDICU-LOUS!

YOUR ANCESTORS REFUSED TO ACCEPT THAT, AND THAT IS WHY THEY WIPED US DEMONS OUT.
SO TYPICAL...
HOW YOU HUMANS LOVE TO DESTROY NATURE.
SHUT UP...
BUT HOW?
IF THE DEMONS WERE TRULY WIPED OUT...
YOU CAN THANK A FOOLISH HUMAN. SOME RESEARCHER...

HE DUG UP OUR BONES.
AND RESURRECTED US USING HIS WORTHLESS TECHNOLOGY.
BECAUSE HE WANTED TO CREATE "THE ULTIMATE LIVING WEAPON OF MASS DESTRUCTION"!
BECAUSE OF WEAPONS ?!
YES.
AND FOR THEIR WEAPONS, WE WERE...

WE WERE HORRIBLY TORTURED. WHO KNOWS HOW MANY OF US...
ROAR RRRRRRR!!!
ROOOW!!
...SUFFERED HUMILIATION AND EXCRUCIATING PAIN.
ALL BEFORE THEY WERE MURDERED IN THE NAME OF MILITARY SCIENCE.

YOU'RE A HALF-BREED, TAINTED BY HUMANITY. YOU DON'T DESERVE IT.
SHE'S NO HALF-BREED!
TAKERU IS HUMAN!
NO... SHE IS A DEMON!

UH...
MOVING ON...
RETURN THE WITCHBLADE TO US, GIRL.
AFTER ALL, IT BELONGED TO US FIRST.

SO TO SHOW OUR GRATITUDE, WE HAVE GIVEN BACK TO HIM WHAT HE GAVE US.
SUFFERING AND PAIN.
SO WE WILL CONTINUE TO EAT MASTER HOUGEN FOR ETERNITY.
ISN'T THAT RIGHT, MASTER HOUGEN?

OH, GAKURA...
I'M SORRY FOR BRINGING UP SUCH PAINFUL MEMORIES.
BUT...
I THOUGHT YOU SAID THAT HOUGEN WAS THE ONE WHO RESURRECTED YOU.
YES, THAT'S RIGHT.

THAT'S RIGHT,. ASK MASTER HOUGEN, WHO IMPREGNATED HIS OWN WIFE WITH DEMON DNA.
WHAT?
HIS WIFE...
...WHOM HE GAVE THE WITCHBLADE TO.
WHAT ?!
UGH...
OH, GOODNESS... IT IS AS I FEARED.
UNGH ....

THAT MAN... IS MY DAUGHTER'S...
HE'S MY DAUGHTER AKENO'S HUSBAND.
HE MUST HAVE HOPED THAT THE CHILD BORN TO HER WOULD BECOME A WITCHBLADE BEARER.
UNFORTUNATELY FOR HIS WIFE, SHE MUST HAVE FOUND OUT MUCH LATER.

HEY MOMMY...
WHY DID YOU NAME ME TAKERU? IT'S ME A BOY'S NAME.
IS IT BETTER TO BE A BOY?
NO DEAR... IT'S BECAUSE GIRLS BECOME DEMONS.
MY CHILD....
YOU MUST *NEVER* GO NEAR THE DEMON'S HAND.

IT'S ABSOLUTELY PERVERSE, ISN'T IT?! THAT HE WOULD CREATE SUCH A BASTARD DEMON-CHILD.
NO HUMAN BEING COULD KNOWINGLY STAND SUCH A THING.
BEARING SUCH AN UNNATURAL CHILD.
OH...
MOMMY...
I'M... HUMAN AND DEMON...
I'M A MON-STER.
THAT'S A HORRIBLE THING...
BUT NOW I KNOW WHY AKENO SUFFERED DEARLY WHILE GIVING BIRTH TO TAKERU-CHAN.
IT'S MY FAULT...
BECAUSE I'M A... DEMON.
TAKERU!
MY MOTHER WAS...
OH...

LADY FUURA, THIS GIRLS' POWERS ARE UNIMAGINABLE. SHE MUST JOIN US–
NO.
NO CREATURE WITH EVEN A DROP OF HUMAN BLOOD MAY JOIN US. NOR ANYONE WHO COULD HAVE DONE THIS TO YOU.
SHE MUST PAY.
WOOSH!

MASTER HOUGEN...
I GIVE THANKS FOR WHAT I AM ABOUT TO CONSUME.
SPLUNK!!!
BA-DUM... BA-DUM
UNGHHHHHHHH...
NOW...
LET'S PUT AN END TO ALL OF THIS.

CHOMP!
SLURP!

T-TAKERU!!!
TAKE GRANNY AND RUN!

GET UP, TAKERU!
TAKERU!
WHAT'S WRONG ?!
GRIP!
GO!
THUK
THUK
THUK
CLANG!

DAD, LISTEN TO ME!
YOU NEED TO GET THEM OUT OF HERE, NOW!
RIGHT!
YOUR HAND...
HOW UNUSUAL...
GRIPPPPPPP!
SISTER SENSHUU-NI! TAKERU-CHAN!
WE MUST GO...
HURRY!
Uhngg...
OH!

TAKERU
!!!

SKREE-
THUNK!
GRANNY!!!

TAKERU...
YOU MUST... GET A HOLD OF YOURSELF...
YOU ARE HUMAN...
YOU ARE... AKENO'S DAUGHTER....
YOU ARE MY GRAND...
OH NO...

MY, MY...
WHAT A BEAUTIFUL DISPLAY OF LOVE.
ズル
SLUMP
GRAND...
...MA?!
AAAAAAAAAAAAHHHHHHH!!
RRRRRRRRRRRRRRRR
WHIRRRRRRR

WOOOOOOOOOSH!
TAKERU ?!
KA-BOOM!!!

SKREEEE-!
PUTT PUTT PUTT
HI.. HI..
OH, MY... WHAT'S GOING ON?

TAKERU?

UNGH...
TAKERU-CHAN, SHE'S CHANGED...
WHAT IS THAT?!
Chapter 9 THE ANNIHILATION

THE WITCH-BLADE...
HOW SAD...
TO BE WASTED ON SOMEONE LIKE YOU.
KREE...
I'LL KILL YOU !!!

AAAAAYYY!!!!!!
TAKERU...

I SEE...
CONTINUE MONITORING HER.
IT SEEMS SHE MAY REACH THE FINAL STAGE OF EVOLUTION EVEN SOONER THAN EXPECTED.
LET'S PUT THE F-18s ON STANDBY.

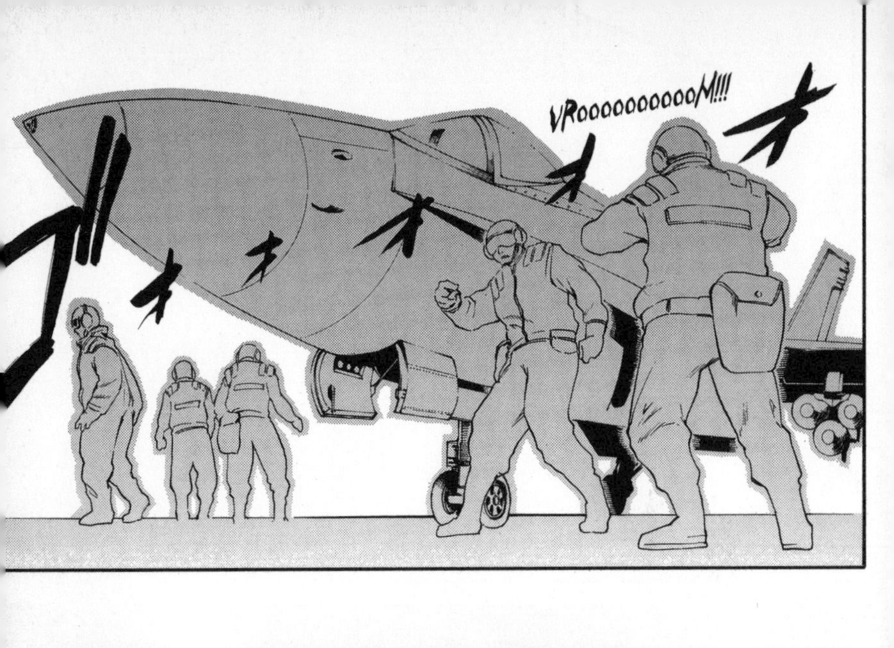
VROOOOOOOOOOM!!!

CLANG
CLANG
CLANG
CLANG
SO THAT'S WHAT THIS WAS ALL ABOUT...
THE DEPUTY SECRETARY NEVER WANTED THE WITCHBLADE. HE WANTS THE BEARER!

ONLY WHEN IT FINDS IT'S TRUE BEARER DOES THE COMPLETE WITCHBLADE POWER MANIFEST.
AND ONLY THEN DOES IT BECOME THE ULTIMATE WEAPON.
TO THINK THAT HE'D EVEN COMMIT MILITARY FORCES TO THIS...
THIS ISN'T SOME LITTLE BATTLE WITH DEMONS...

THIS IS LIKE WAGING WORLD WAR THREE.
Gulp!

I SAID STEP ON IT!
SKREEEEEEEEEECH!
WE HAVE TO GET A HOLD OF THE WITCHBLADE BEFORE IT'S TOO LATE!

WHOA!!!
THUMP
THUMP
THUMP
HUH ?!

WOOSH!
FWOP!
FWIP!

GAAAAAAAAAAAAAAAH!!!
SMACK!

BUMP
BUMP
BUMP
LADY FUURA!
I'M FINE.

BUT YOU...
HOW CAN YOU LET YOUR ANGER GET THE BEST OF YOU LIKE THAT?
I'M SORRY...
I SHOULD NO BETTER THAN TO STOOP SO LOW.

PLEASE MY LADY...
THROW ME AT HER.
LET ME DO MY PART.
GAKURA...
WHEN THIS IS OVER, I WILL MAKE YOU WHOLE AGAIN.

TAKERU...
DAMN IT!
ONCE AGAIN I'M HELPLESS.
NO, KOU.
THERE IS SOMETHING YOU CAN DO. REMEMBER?
HONOR-ING...
THAT LEFT HAND OF YOURS.
DAD...

I'M GOING TO EVACUATE THE REST OF THE VILLAGERS.
BEFORE THE MILITARY ARRIVES.
TAKERU?
HOW CAN I HELP?

HOW STRANGE...
MASTER GAKURA SHOULD BE BACK BY NOW.
WHAT WAS THAT FLASH?!
LADY FUURA?!
SOME-THING'S HAPPENED DOWN THERE!
LET'S GO.

WHY CAN'T I GO INTO THE VILLAGE?
MY FRIENDS ARE DOWN THERE!
YOU DON'T KNOW WHEN TO GIVE UP!
IF YOU DON'T GET OUT OF HERE--
WHACK!
WHUMP!

THUMP!
IF YOU KNOW WHAT'S GOOD FOR YOU, GO HOME! MAKE YOURSELF A SANDWICH AND FORGET ABOUT THIS!
CLANGGGG!
THUD!
Ooooooh...

HURRY!
WE HAVE GET CLEAR OF THE VILLAGE!!
GAACK ....
DOCTOR... WHAT IN THE ...
WHAT IN THE WORLD IS HAPPENING ?!
HONESTLY, I CAN HARDLY BELIEVE IT MYSELF...

オォォォォ オォォォ
VRRRRoooooooooMMMMM!!!!
ALL HELL IS GONNA BREAK LOOSE. HOW ARE YOU GOING TO EXPLAIN THIS TO THE JAPANESE GOVERNMENT.
EASY. JAPAN HAD THIS HEROIC DEMON HUNTER CALLED CHERRY BOY—NO WAIT, *PEACH* BOY.
BUT HE WAS DESTROYED IN THE JAPAN-U.S. SECURITY TREATY. SO ALL WE'RE DOING IS STEPPING UP TO TAKE HIS PLACE.

THIS ISN'T RIGHT.
THAT'S OKAY. MOMMY WILL UNDERSTAND.
CLANG!
WHRRRRRRR
DAMN IT! WHAT CAN I DO?!

WHIPP!
I'VE GOT YOU!
GRRRPPP!
YOU THINK SO?
WOOOOSHH

TAKERU!
THUD!
THUD!
THUD!
THUD!

TAKER-
UUNGH!
KOU?!
KOU?!
GAKURA...

SNIK-
BLAM!
AAAAAAAAAH!

WHUMP!
MUST...
KILL...
GET AWAY...
YOU'RE NOT WORTHY OF KILLING GAKURA.

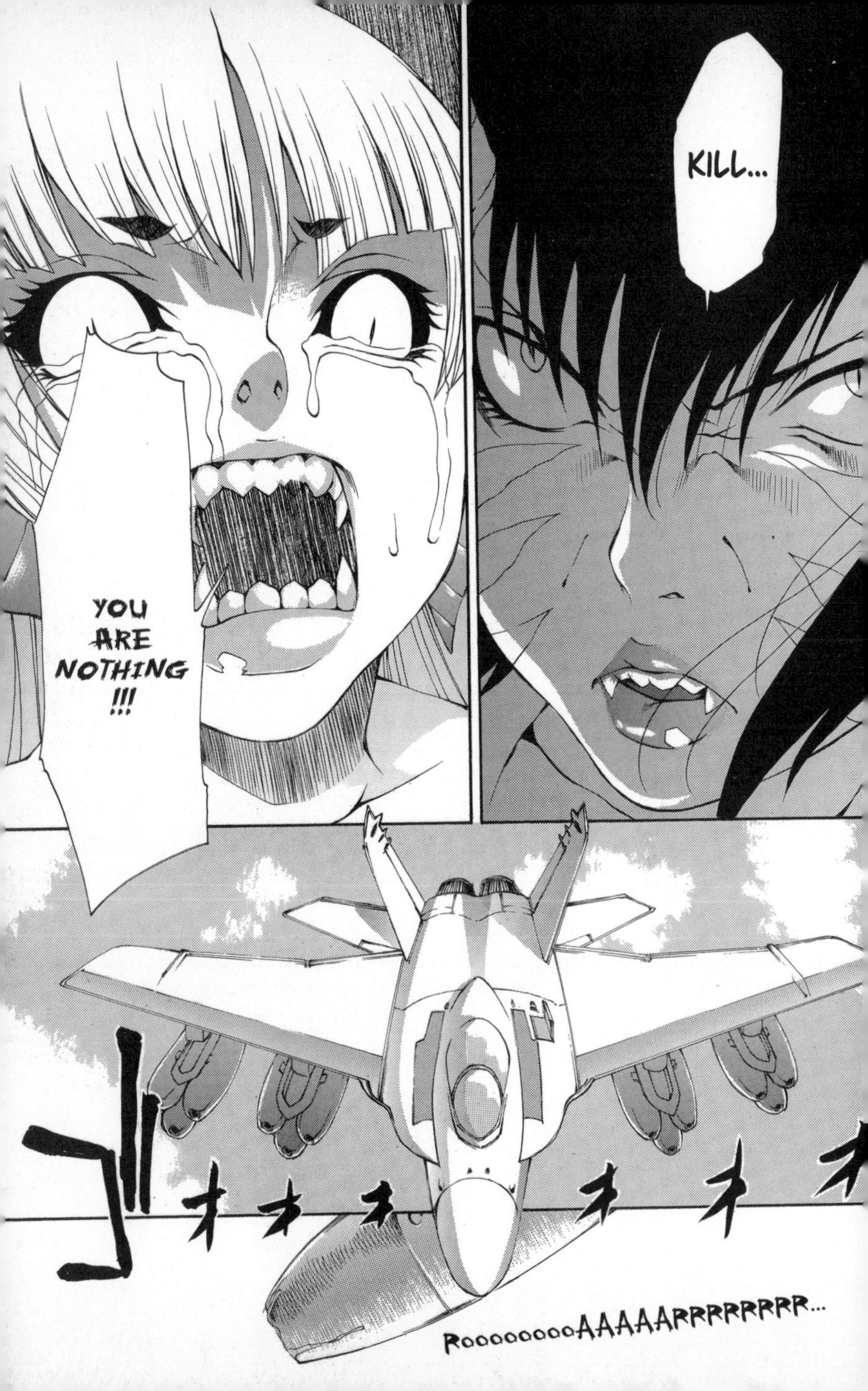
KILL...
YOU ARE NOTHING !!!
ゴオオオオオオ
RoooooooooAAAAARRRRRRRR...

BooM!!!!
NO!
IT'S THEM. THE...
THE AMERICAN FORCES!

THooooooM!!!
AAARGH!!!
BooM
BooM
BooM

AM I NOW SUPPOSED TO BELIEVE THAT WE ARE POWERLESS?
THAT OUR RESURRECTION WAS JUST A FANTASY...
A DREAM WE ARE WAKING UP FROM...

KA-THOOM!!!
LADY FUURA!!!
WE'VE.... FAILED...
PLEASE... RUN AWAY!!!
FAILED YOU...

BOOM
BOOM
BOOM
KA-DOOOOOOM!!!
RoAAAAAAAARRRRRRRRR!!!

UNGH...
NO...
WHOOOM!!!!
GAKURA... THE FOREST....
OUR HOMELAND... THE ONE WE DREAMED OF.... IT'S BURNING DOWN BEFORE OUR EYES.

IT'S ALL...

JUST A DREAM...

THE VILLAGE AND THE DEMONS...
IT'S ALL BURNED DOWN.
OH...
UNGH...
NO...
NO NO NO...

NOOOOOOOOOOOOOOO!!!
AAAAAAAAAHHHH!
TAKERU!!!

RooooooooARRRRR....
RRRooooAAAARRRRRRRRRRRRRR
TAKERU ?!

TAKERU, WATCH YOUR STEP...
PROMISE ME THAT YOU'LL KEEP THIS AS OUR LITTLE SECRET, OKAY?
LOOK!
WOW!

Chapter 10 TRUTH REVEALED

KOU...
THIS PLACE... SOME MAY THINK IT'S JUST SOME QUAINT LITTLE VILLAGE...
BUT NOT ME...
I LOVE IT.

GRANDMA AND SISTER SEISHUU ARE ALL HERE...
YOU'RE HERE... YOUR FATHER TOO.
AND ALL MY MEMORIES OF MY MOTHER– THE SHORT TIME WE HAD TOGETHER, IT WAS ALL HERE.
IF I COULD...
I WOULD STAY HERE FOREVER.
UNBELIEV-ABLE.
I CAN'T BELIEVE THEY WENT THIS FAR...

KOU-
WHY... WHY?!
SHE... TAKERU DIDN'T DO ANYTHING WRONG!!!
SHE WAS JUST A PRETTY GIRL IN HIGH SCHOOL.
WHY DID THIS HAVE TO HAPPEN TO HER?!
Grrrrp!
WHY?!
THUK!
GRIPPPP!
UNGH!!!
KOU...
YOUR HAND?!

SPLOOOOOOOOSH!
WHAT?! THE WITCHBLADE BEARER HAS DISAPPEARED?!
SLAM!
HEY!
HOW DARE YOU GO OUT TO RUN AN ERRAND FOR MOMMY, AND COME BACK EMPTY HANDED?!
FIND THAT GIRL... NOW!
INCOMPETENT FOOL...
IS IT POSSIBLE THAT SHE WAS CAUGHT IN THE BOMBING?! MAYBE SHE-
IMPOSSIBLE!
IF THE WITCHBLADE COULD BE DESTROYED SO EASILY, WE WOULDN'T BE GOING THROUGH ALL THIS DAMNED TROUBLE!!!
FINE. NO NEED TO YELL...

BUT STILL, WHERE IN THE WORLD IS THAT LITTLE LADY...
PLAYING HIDE AND SEEK, PERHAPS?
SPLASH
SPLASH
SPLASH

GRRRRRRR...

I SEE...
I HAD NO IDEA TAKERU-CHAN HAD SUCH A PAST...
NOW I UNDERSTAND WHY THE WITCHBLADE CHOSE HER.
SHE IS HUMAN.
IT MAKES NO DIFFERENCE IF SHE HAD DEMON BLOOD IN HER. IF IT WEREN'T FOR THE DAMNED WITCHBLADE...
DAMN IT!! CAN'T WE DO ANY-THING?!
THE WITCHBLADE WILL ONLY LEAVE HER... WHEN SHE DIES.
NO...

TRYING TO FORCE IT OFF OF HER WILL ONLY INCAPACITATE HER... OR WORSE, KILL HER.
THE WITCHBLADE TURNS THE BEARER INTO PURE INSTINCT. TAKERU HAS NO WILL OF HER OWN. SHE IS CONSUMED WITH KILLING...
...AND NO ONE CAN STOP THAT NOW.

HUH?!
WHAT IS IT?
UHM, DEPUTY SECRETARY... WE, ARE, UHM...
DEPUTY SECRETARY!!! THE ENTERPRISE IS UNDER ATTACK!
I CAN SEE THAT!!!
WHAT HAPPENED?! AND MORE IMPORTANTLY, WHO IS ATTACKING THEM?!

IT CAN'T BE–
IT IS.
IT HAS TO BE.
THE WITCHBLADE BEARER HAS COME FOR REVENGE.
THAT'S IMPOS-SIBLE.
THERE'S NO OTHER EXPLAN-ATION.
SHE IS HERE, LAYING SIEGE TO A THE ENTIRE U.S. FLEET.
IMPRESSIVE.

WE HAVE ORDERS TO ATTACK!!! RETURN FIRE!
AGAINST... THAT?!
DO IT!
THERE ORDERS COME DIRECTLY FROM THE DEPUTY SECRETARY!
WHAT ARE WE SUPPOSED TO USE AGAINST HER?! ANTI-PERSONAL WEAPONS ARE--

MISS SAKURAI!
WE'VE GOT SERIOUS TROUBLE!
THE WITCHBLADE BEARER HAS ENGAGED THE U.S. FORCES IN THE PACIFIC!
HUH?
YOU CAN'T BE SERIOUS... CAN YOU?!
GET A CHOPPER READY, RIGHT NOW! I'M GOING OVER THERE!
WAIT! ME TOO!

PLEASE,... YOU CAN'T LEAVE ME HERE. TAKE ME WITH YOU!

WUP
WUP
WUP
WUP
WUP

IS THAT... TAKERU-CHAN'S SKIN THAT'S GRAFTED TO YOUR HAND?!

DON'T WORRY, KOU. NO MATTER WHAT HAPPENS...
I'LL RESTORE YOU, BACK THE WAY YOU WERE.

YES. SHE'S SO BEAU-TIFUL...
YET SHE THOUGHT NOTHING OF SCARRING UP HER BODY FOR MY SAKE.

MAYBE I HAVE MORE THAN JUST TAKERU'S FLESH ON MY HAND.
AND IF IT WILL LET ME HELP HER IN SOME WAY, SO BE IT!
I DON'T CARE WHAT HAPPENS TO ME!
TAKERU...
I'LL DO ANY-THING FOR YOU.

KOU-KUN...

ANYTHING.
YOU'LL NEVER BE ALONE, TAKERU.
WE'VE LOST CONTACT WITH THE ENTER-PRISE.
THE REAGAN IS CURRENTLY ENGAGED!
GUNSHIP #16... HAS GONE SILENT, TOO!
WE JUST LOST CONTACT WITH THEM !
SIR... WE'VE LOST CONTACT WITH THE TWO FLEETS DEPLOYED TO OUR BOW.
WE'RE THE LAST ONES LEFT!
THAT'S NOT POSSI-BLE!
YOU'RE TALKING ABOUT THE UNITED STATES NAVY!

DEPUTY SECRETARY...
THE CHOPPER IS READY!
WHAT?!
WE'RE SITTING DUCK OUT HERE.
WITH NO PROTECTION, IT'S JUST A MATTER OF TIME BEFORE THE BEARER COMES FOR US.
BOOM!
NO!

ゴゴゴ
RUMBLE RUMBLE BOOM!
WE LOST SHIP #21!
BUT HOW?!

TAKERU!
LET'S GO... YOU'VE GOT TO FLY LOWER!
BUT THE U.S. FORCES MIGHT ATTACK.
YES, MA'AM.
THEY'VE GOT MORE IMPORTANT THINGS TO WORRY ABOUT!

THERE SHE IS!!!
Final Chapter A SHOW OF POWER PART 2

TAKERU!
JUMP!
THE DEVAS-TATION...
IT'S NOT LIKE HER TO DO THIS! WHY?!
TAKERU...

THUMP
CLANK!
HEY! KOU?!
TAKERU!!! STOP THIS!!
LOOK OUT!
GET A HOLD OF YOURSELF!
TAKERU!!!
HUH?

WAAASH
THUD!

SHIP #21 IS EVACUATING IT'S CREW!
NO SIGN OF THE ENEMY!
IMPOSSIBLE. SHE IS HERE.
RIGHT BEFORE OUR EYES!!!
GULP!

BOOM!
Ooomph!!
AIRCRAFT'S 310 AND 313 HAVE BEEN DOWNED!
UNGH...
DEPUTY SECRETARY, ARE YOU OKAY?

SOMEBODY... STOP HER!!
NO... KILL HER!

SOME-BODY... ANY-BODY... KILL HER!
OH, NO...
MOM...
HELP ?!

MOMMY, HELP...
MOMMY-
WHIRRRRRRRRRRRR
TAKERU!

TAKERU...
STOP!
HUH?!
YOU'VE GOT TO STOP...
LET'S GO HOME... TOGETHER...
HOME?

YES, HOME...
LET'S GO BACK TO OUR VILLAGE!
KOU...
OOO-MPH!
TAKERU...
KOU...
YOU PROMISED ME...
REMEMBER?

THAT IF I... BECAME A DEMON...
YOU PROMISED YOU'D... KILL ME...
I DID...
BUT TAKERU, YOU'RE HUMAN!!!
I CAN'T...
CAN'T STOP ...
PLEASE...
KILL ME.
TAKERU!
K...KOU...

MY LEFT HAND...
I'LL USE IT... FOR YOUR SAKE...
PLEASE...
GRIPPP

KOU...
THANK
YOU...

IT'S OVER. BUDDHA PROTECT US. WE'VE PAID A STEEP PRICE.
LET'S GO..

TAKERU...

IT'S BEEN A YEAR, BUT NOT MUCH HAS CHANGED.
SHE STILL CAN'T WALK... AND SHE HASN'T SAID A WORD.
SIGH

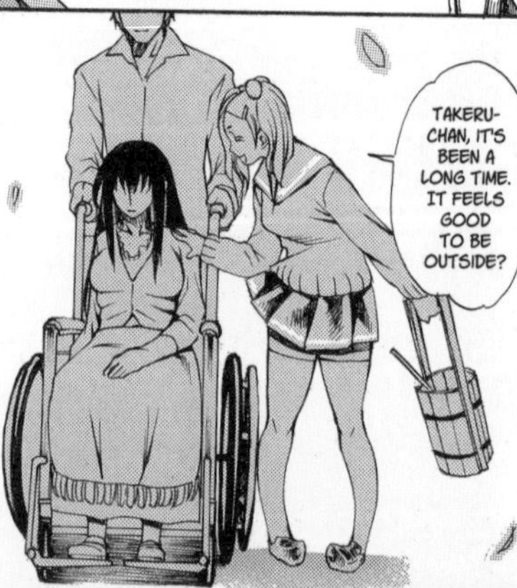
IN THE AFTERMATH, THE AMERICANS OFFICIALLY CALLED THE INCIDENT... "AN ACCIDENT." THE CASE IS CLASSIFIED, AND THE WITCHBLADE REMAINS AT THE BOTTOM OF THE PACIFIC.
TAKERU-CHAN, IT'S BEEN A LONG TIME. IT FEELS GOOD TO BE OUTSIDE?
STILL, THE WHOLE THING LEAVES A BAD TASTE IN THE MOUTH... DOESN'T IT?

WHAT ARE YOU SUGGESTING ?!
THAT IT'S NOT OVER?
AREN'T THEY PRETTY?
TAKERU-CHAN, FLOWERS!
YOU THINK IT'S JUST A MATTER OF TIME BEFORE THE WITCHBLADE RETURNS?
FLO... WERS-
SOMEHOW... SOMEDAY...
...WELL GET OUR HAPPY ENDING.

WE JUST HAVE TO KEEP UP HOPE.
THE END

AKERU MANGA

KOBAYASHI YASUKO & SUMITA KAZASA

WITCHBLADE
TAKERU

KOBAYASHI YASUKO & SUMITA KAZASA

WITCHBLADE